SYRIA

A LIVING HISTORY

October 15, 2016–February 26, 2017

Five thousand years, one unprecedented partnership: the Aga Khan Museum joins leading public institutions and private collectors to present Syria's rich cultural heritage. *Syria: A Living History* brings together artifacts and artworks that illuminate Syria's cultural diversity, historical continuity, resourcefulness, and resilience.

Under the patronage of
UNESCO

United Nations
Educational, Scientific and
Cultural Organization

In partnership with

United Nations
Educational, Scientific and
Cultural Organization

Organisation
des Nations Unies
pour l'éducation,
la science et la culture

Canadian
Commission
for UNESCO

Commission
canadienne
pour l'UNESCO

SYRIA
A LIVING HISTORY

AGA KHAN MUSEUM

TABLE OF CONTENTS

FOREWORD

Syria: A Living History is an exhibition brought to life through a partnership of eight international institutions which have felt compelled to tell the remarkable history of Syria during these troubled times. Presented under the patronage of UNESCO, it reflects a true universal outpouring of support for the artistic and cultural history of the region.

Today, Syria is a country in the global spotlight, associated with stories of conflict, raging wars and mass migration of people seeking refuge. There is another story of Syria — one ignored by current media coverage — and it tells of a resilient country and creative peoples, reflecting a rich history of multiculturalism.

Syria has a history that spans many millennia and is a region that houses two of the world's oldest continuously inhabited cities — Damascus and Aleppo. It has also served as a home to and, in turn, been influenced by countless world civilizations, including Babylonian, Hittite, Greek, Roman, Byzantine, Sasanian, Mamluk, Ottoman and Arab.

This indomitable legacy is reflected through the artifacts presented in this exhibition, which range from masterpieces carved by ancient Syrian peoples, to artworks created by present-day artists and artisans. From a gypsum eye idol from Tell Brak (ca. 3200 BCE) to a painting by Fateh al-Moudarres (one of the leaders of the modern Syrian art movement), the interplay of Syrian cultures and history reveal themselves through the country's art.

The importance of Syria's contribution to world heritage has never been in doubt. Despite the destruction that has taken place in conflict zones, the spirit of the Syrian past can and will be restored, led by organizations such as UNESCO and the Aga Khan Trust for Culture which played prominent roles in the restoration of monuments in Syria prior to the war.

The Aga Khan Museum wishes to thank the Musée du Louvre, Paris; the Museum of Islamic Art, Berlin; the Vorderasiatisches Museum, Berlin; the Metropolitan Museum of Art, New York; the Royal Ontario Museum, Toronto; the Atassi Foundation, Dubai; and the Marshall and Marilyn R. Wolf, Toronto for their outstanding leadership in providing loans of objects to the exhibition. It would also like to thank Professor Nasser Rabbat for co-curating this exhibition and Dr. Ross Burns for his insightful guidance during the project.

Henry S. Kim
Director and CEO, Aga Khan Museum

Hall of the Knights
Krak de Chevaliers
Ayyubid and Crusader Periods
Image Courtesy of Ross Burns

SYRIA: WHERE CULTURES MET

WHAT CAN WE SAY ABOUT SYRIA TODAY? A country that has for centuries enjoyed a unique mosaic of ethnicities, cultures, religions, and sects has been reduced in six years of senseless factional war to brutally divided fiefs, ruined cities and towns, and scorched landscape. Much has been lost for good and it will take the dedicated and selfless work of at least a generation or two to restore what is left.

In these painful times, however, it is crucial to counter and debunk the forces of destruction and erasure of memory. One way is to celebrate the land and its people, highlight their heritage, and emphasize the cultural continuity and diversity that has shaped their long history and endowed them with an intricate, multi-layered, yet not easily bracketed notion of self.

Slowly taking shape out of Assyria, Aram, and Phoenicia before becoming Seleukia, then Roman and Byzantine Syria, Islamic Bilad al-Sham, and finally the truncated modern Syria, the country has assimilated many interrelated cultures. Some flourished for a long time and radiated their influence near and far. Others shone brightly for a brief, intense moment before retreating to the realm of memory. Still others inhabited small niches in the land and evolved quietly to emerge as unique expressions of particularly Syrian cultural medleys. All, however, contributed to the rich landscape of Syria and gave it its vivid multiculturalism long before the term itself was coined.

This expansive and diverse cultural topography is what the Aga Khan Museum is aspiring to capture in this exhibition, *Syria: A Living History*. By bringing together beautiful artifacts carefully selected from several partner museums and collections and dating from the fourth millennium BCE to the present, the museum aims to showcase Syria's long history of eloquent, varied, and multi-layered artistic creativity. Photographs of major monuments and landscape, also spanning the country's long history, amplify the message.

FACING PAGE:

Qasr Ibn Wardan Church
Late Antiquity
Image courtesy of Ross Burns

An additional goal is to alert the public to the damage sustained by many of them and the efforts of numerous organizations to document their remains, preserve their memory, and even recreate them in 3-D models.

Despite its emphasis on history and continuity, the exhibition has been conceived around a number of ideas that can be traced across the many periods and cultures of Syrian history and are part of a universally shared locus of culture. These include the changing relationships between people and the divine as beliefs transitioned from a crowded pantheon to one God; the way in which people interacted with nature and it bounties and menaces; the way that organized states relied upon religion, hierarchy and symbolism to maintain order; the idea of home, as a shelter and the centre of an individual's world—which have been subjects of representation in all cultures and at all times.

Thus, the artifacts presented under these headings are meant to underscore the universality of their shapes, functions, and intents as well as the particularities of their Syrian environment, inspiration, and sensibilities and their artistic contribution to world culture. Two last sections round out the exhibit and bring it to the present. The first, "Affinities," pairs objects from different times and locations in order to reveal the cultural continuity that motivated the similarities in their forms and feels. The second, "Vagaries of the Time," reminds us of what is happening in Syria now and exposes the grave threats to its people, land, and heritage. But the show ends on a note of luminous hope. This is indeed the feeling that we want the visitor to leave with: hope for a better future for Syria and its people and hope for art and culture as enduring beacons of humanism.

Nasser Rabbat
Aga Khan Professor, MIT
Director of the Aga Khan Program for Islamic Architecture

SYRIA'S ARCHITECTURE

GIVEN THE TRAGIC EVENTS that have reduced much of Syria's habitat and cultural landscape to rubble over the past five years, this important exhibition will serve as a reminder of what the world owes to Syria in the sheer richness, variety and continuity of its heritage across millennia.

Visitors to Syria before 2011 could let the experience of its diverse civilizations sink in via the luxury of leisurely visits, moving from Bronze Age excavations, via the great columned avenues of Apamea or through the literally hundreds of Byzantine villages and churches scattered among the limestone hills west of Aleppo. Travel further inland brought more wonders, such as the beautiful Byzantine manor house and church at Qasr Ibn Wardan or the remote Roman temple at Isriya, stranded in the parched reaches of the steppe. The dark obdurate basalt of the Hauran had yielded to the skills of the local craftsmen who, over centuries, fashioned the Classical and Islamic buildings found in an extraordinarily fluid style scattered across scores of sites in Southern Syria.

As one moved from temple to church, to fortress or mosque, from Roman theatre to Islamic baths, a kaleidoscope of cultures became almost too much to absorb. The importance of Syria's historical treasures, however, and the way they came to be presented in recent decades, taught the world some new lessons. No culture simply dominated or trashed its predecessor; each era developed a dominant 'style' but they all learned from each other—borrowed ideas, recycled stones, used the old temples and basilicas anew, or deployed signature elements such as columns, niches, arches or porticos in new ways. In addition, some historical eras, which had simply been a 'black hole' in our understanding of the past, were enlightened by major discoveries in Syria, such as Bronze Age Ebla, which opened a completely new perspective on what had been a puzzling millennium.

Today, sadly, we can only provide a sample of the buildings and sites through the objects shown in this exhibition that have been unearthed from the ruins of Babylonian, Hittite, Aramaean, Roman or Byzantine buildings or which once graced the homes and castles of the Umayyads, Seljuks or of the later Islamic dynasties that based their empires on Syria—Zengids, Ayyubids and Mamluks—and finally the Ottomans.

No other country in the Middle East can document this parade of cultures so completely as Syria. The researchers who devoted their careers to recording these remains worked prodigiously to show how these cultures were interlocked. Sites such as Palmyra, which were once seen as simply yielding Classical throw-backs for the pattern books of eighteenth century European architects, have, in the last fifty years, begun to show a much richer range of cultures—Byzantine churches, rare examples of early Umayyad buildings (mosque, suqs), an Ayyubid castle and a Mamluk fortified bastion.

As a result of the work of Syrian and foreign researchers, the clearest lessons for the visitor was that most of these places had remained living cities that absorbed influences from a mosaic of patrons, visitors, travelling architects and artisans. As you move around the exhibition today, Syria's present-day tragedy and the suffering of its people will be on your mind. It will be hard to imagine any country coming through this harrowing experience without deep and disabling scars. When Syria does manage to put this ordeal behind it, the memory of its complex and interlocking past will be part of the basis for its revival.

Ross Burns
Historian, *Syria: a Living History* Consultant

EXHIBITION HIGHLIGHTS

Eye Idol

Small figurines known as eye idols were probably presented at temples as votive offerings for spiritual protection. This example was excavated at Tell Brak in northeastern Syria, one of the world's earliest ancient cities, where thousands of eye idols were found in a building that has been named the "Eye Temple." Eye idols can be found in various sizes; some, like this one, have multiple sets of carved eyes, some have jewelry and some are represented with a child. Believed to be related to Egyptian and Mesopotamian cultures, this powerful symbol was traditionally thought to offer protection against the evil eye.

Tell Brak, Syria, ca. 3200 BCE
Ancient Mesopotamian Period
Gypsum, carved

On loan from the Royal Ontario Museum, 959.91.50

Stele with Depiction of a Prayer

One of the most fascinating personalities of the late 19th and early 20th centuries was Baron Max von Oppenheim. After his diplomatic service, he devoted himself to studying Bedouin culture and, as an archaeologist, he explored Tell Halaf, in northeastern Syria, a site dating from the Neolithic period. The city was also part of Hittite, Aramaean and Assyrian civilizations. Oppenheim's finds were displayed at the Tell Halaf Museum in Berlin, opened to the public in 1930. In 1943, aerial bombing destroyed almost all the limestone sculptures, a large number of small finds and the plaster reconstructions. In the 1990's, the surviving fragments were entrusted to Berlin's State Museums as a long-term loan on condition that the fragments would be restored and displayed again.

Excavated in the sanctuary at Tell Halaf, this Syrian-Aramaic dedicatory stele with a relief of a worshipper, has faced many dangers through the centuries and survived the vagaries of time.

Tell Halaf, Syria, 10th–9th century BCE
Archaic Period
Basalt, carved

Vorderasiatisches Museum, TH B 4871

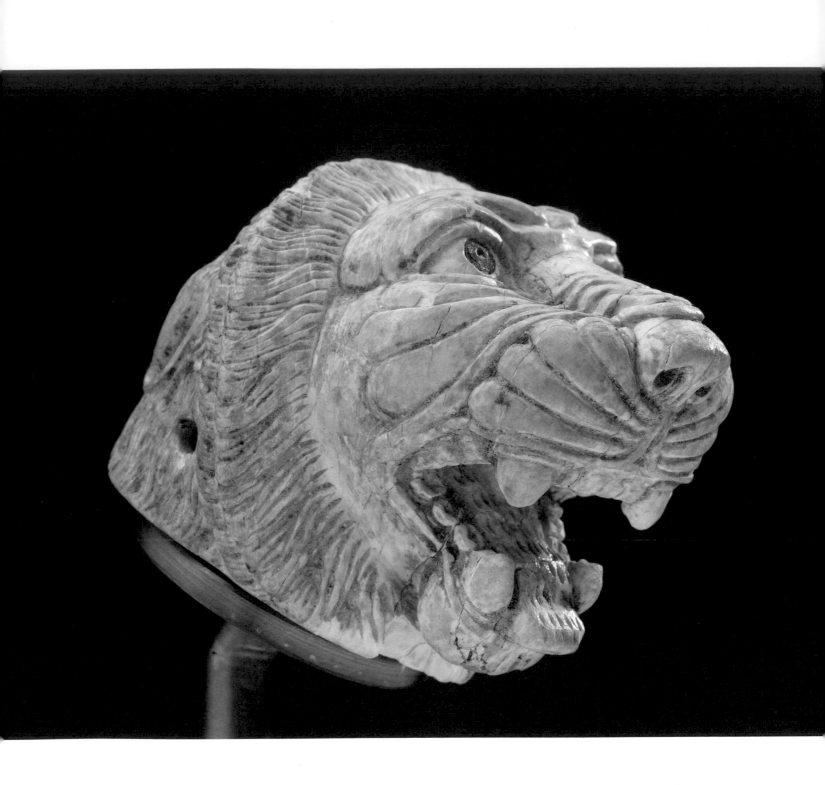

Lion's Head

Scholars have not identified the original function of this exquisite ivory head of a male lion. It may have been the finial of a chair's armrest. The dynamic action of its opened mouth, exposing dangerous canines and taut facial muscles, suggests its readiness to attack. Despite its small dimensions, this lion is part of the same Near Eastern tradition as the colossal sculptures of lions that symbolize kingship and power. The material of this artwork is also significant: in ancient civilizations, from Anatolia to Syria and Egypt, artists modelled ivory from the tusks of elephants and hippopotami, wild boar and sea cows.

Historic Syria, 9th–8th centuries BCE
Archaic Period
Ivory, carved

On loan from the Royal Ontario Museum, 996.86.1

Bowl

Syria has a very old tradition of glass making as part of its material culture, based on Roman and early Christian examples and techniques. The composite mosaic glass technique called millefiori (Italian, meaning thousand flowers) used in this bowl was well known and highly popular in Roman society. This labor intensive and very time-consuming technique also flourished during the early Islamic period, especially during the Abbasid Caliphate after they took control of Syria in the 8th century. The Islamic pieces tend to imitate the Roman style.

This Roman example from Homs shows the mosaic pattern formed by polygonal sections of two canes of glass: one has a purple ground outlined in white; the second has a blue green ground with a spoked circle of yellow dots and a central white dot.

Probably Homs, Syria, 25 BCE–25 CE
Classical Period
Glass, mosaic

Lent by The Metropolitan Museum of Art, Rogers Fund, 1912 (12.212.1)

Tomb Relief

Palmyra was an exceptional city-state and a major trade emporium that controlled trade routes from Mesopotamia and beyond to the Mediterranean between the 1st century BCE and the 3rd century CE. Located in an oasis in the middle of the Syrian desert, the city developed a syncretic architectural and artistic tradition that combined classical—Hellenistic and Roman—elements with Syrian, Mesopotamian, and Persian forms, techniques, and practices. Most notable is its unique funerary architecture: tomb-towers containing stratified rows of personal stone coffins running along the internal walls and fronted by carved reliefs of the deceased's bust or of a more animated family scene.

The relief shown here is a typical example, with the bust of Tiklak, daughter of Aphshi, whose name and genealogy are incised on each side of her head in Palmyrene Aramaic. Dressed in a classical tunic, pinned by a brooch with a cloak draped over her head and shoulders, Tiklak smiles and calmly looks ahead, past her viewer, into some unknown distance. She holds her gown with her right hand in a gesture common to Palmyra's funerary reliefs, while her left hand clutches some unknown objects, perhaps spindles. Her adornment is minimal in comparison to other Palmyrene reliefs, consisting of a ring, a pair of earrings, and a headband, possibly indicating modesty or a middle-class background.

Palmyra, Syria, 123
Classical Period
Limestone, carved

On loan from the Royal Ontario Museum, 953X94.1

Fragment of a Floor Mosaic

When Syria became a province of the Roman Empire in 64 BCE, there were mutual influences on both civilizations. Mosaic, the art of covering an architectural surface with small, colourful elements—pebbles, stones or glass—for decorative and practical purposes, dates back to the 3rd millennium BCE. Mesopotamia and Greece were particularly renowned for their mosaic panels, a technique which was further enhanced in Roman and Byzantine periods; using smaller mosaic pieces resulted in more detailed designs and more realistic figures. The same technique was favoured in the Sasanian Empire and during the early Islamic period as well when many artists from the Byzantine Empire were commissioned to produce these mosaics.

This mosaic fragment, once part of a house or villa in the city of Daphne, a popular Roman resort residence outside the city of Antioch in today's Turkey, consists of five rows of parrots on a white background. The parrot type, later known as the Alexandrian Parrot, was named after Alexander the Great, who introduced this Indian species to Mediterranean and European territories.

Daphne (near Antioch),
Historic Syria, late 5th–early 6th centuries
Late Antiquity
Stone and cement

The Louvre Museum, Department of Greek, Etruscan, and Roman Antiquities, MA 3459

Two Vases

Pictured at far left, the rounded vase with a straight neck, embossed around the middle with a frieze of medallions containing portraits of biblical figures, is a fine example of metalwork in Byzantine art. Christ is flanked by St. Paul and St. Peter while Mary, on the opposite side, is flanked by two archangels, John the Baptist and presumably John the Evangelist. Such vessels were used as containers for the Eucharist wine. The vase was found in the ruins of a church in Emesa, the ancient city now known as Homs. It became known by scholars as the Emesus Vase.

FACING PAGE, LEFT:

Homs, Syria, late 6th century
Late Antiquity
Silver, hammered, chased and engraved

The Louvre Museum, Department of Greek, Etruscan, and Roman Antiquities, Bj1895

FACING PAGE, RIGHT:

Made for Sultan al-Malik al-Nasir Salah al-Din Yusuf (r. 1236–1260)
Aleppo or Damascus, Syria, 1236–1260
Islamic Period
Copper alloy, hammered, repoussé, chased, and inlaid with silver and black paste

The Louvre Museum, Department of Islamic Art, OA 4090

On the right, this vase is a spectacular example of 13th century Syrian metalwork. Its shape has no parallels in the metalwork of its time and is part of the tradition of ceramic baluster vases. The only existing metalwork similar to this vase is an early Christian work in silver, the so-called Emesus vase. It is adorned on the neck and lower-middle section with inscriptions, which celebrate the ruler of the Ayyubid Dynasty of Syria in Aleppo and Damascus, Sultan al-Nasir Salah al-Din Yusuf (r. 1237–60) who commissioned the piece. The Ayyubid dynasty was founded by Salah al-din, known in the West as Saladin. In addition to the informative inscription, which contains the sultan's titles and a series of votive formulae, the vase follows a dynastic repertoire in design and decoration. Multi lobed medallions feature scenes from courtly life.

A later inscription, added to the base of this vase, reads: "ordered for the cellar of al-Malik al-Zahir," probably referring to the Mamluk Sultan Baybars (r. 1260–1277), the fourth ruler of the dynasty, who conquered Damascus in 1260. This inscription marks the passing of the rule from the Ayyubids to the Mamluks, their former slave-warriors, who took over the sultanate seat in Egypt in 1250. The vase is also known as the Barberini vase, after another owner, Pope Urban VII Barberini, which shows the long lasting interest of European connoisseurs in Islamic metalwork.

Incense burner

With their close kinship to Mosuli (from Mosul, northern Iraq) and Iranian metalworkers of the 12th and 13th centuries, Mamluk artisans developed a stable repertoire of forms, decorations, and techniques, which they continued to hone throughout the 13th, 14th and 15th centuries. Incense burners, or hand warmers, as the Chinese called them, were common in Mamluk metalwork. Most are open-work brass spheres inlaid with gold and silver and decorated with geometric and vegetal patterns, formulaic inscriptions, and, in the early period, stylized figures.

This delicate incense burner belongs to the early Mamluk period. Made of two hemispherical halves, it has a gimbal cup that rotates on a single axis, ensuring that the cup always remained upright. This mechanism is currently known as a "Cardanic suspension," named after the 16th century Italian mathematician Geronimo Cardano. The surface displays many figures that together represent the attributes of royal life: hunting, music, drinking, and furusiyya (equestrianism). A series of saluki hunting dogs run around the rims of both hemispheres and figures of an archer on a horse, a falconer, a seated royal figure with a cup in his hand, and three musicians occupy the six roundels that make up the middle register of both hemispheres. This is an outstanding example of a royal or a princely incense burner even though the absence of a dedicatory inscription on its surface suggests that, despite its high quality, it might have been made commercially and not commissioned by a specific patron.

Syria, 13th century
Islamic Period
Copper alloy, silver and gold, pierced, engraved and inlaid

Museum für Islamische Kunst, MIK I. 2774

Albarello

Albarelli were ceramic vessels used as pharmaceutical jars to transport and store apothecaries' remedies, ointments and dry medicinal herbs. Their incurved cylindrical form, as well as their lack of spouts and handles, are characteristic of vessels that were not intended to contain liquids. The form of these jar types made them easy to hold, use, and shelve. The concave neck and ring-like opening of the *albarello* made it possible to seal it tight with a tied up piece of parchment or similar material.

This *albarello* shows numerous similarities to other examples made in Syria, which were also exported to Europe, evidence of an active trade and exchange beyond the Mediterranean Sea.

Syria, 15th century
Islamic Period
Fritware, underglaze-painted

AKM569

Niche From a Samaritan House

Damascus was a cosmopolitan city during the Mamluk period (1250–1516). Scholars from all over the Islamic world flocked to its numerous institutions of learning, while traders working in Syria, Egypt, the Maghrib, Anatolia, Iran and beyond either passed through it or located their businesses in it. Muslims, Christians, and Jews shared its intra-muros quarters and mingled with each other and with European, African, and Indian traders in its sprawling markets. The wealth of the city and its citizens was most impressively displayed in its splendid, large, and profusely decorated courtyard houses, which nonetheless had plain adobe outer walls. The rich houses of other religious groups did not differ from those of Muslims except in the content and, sometimes, the language of the inscriptions that adorned the friezes, niches, and doors.

This niche comes from the reception hall or *qa'a* of a Jewish Samaritan house that dates from the end of the Mamluk period and its inscriptions are from the Old Testament (Book of Moses: 2 and 5). Otherwise, the niche shape, with its slender rose columns, marble insets of simple geometric shapes, muqarnas conch, and the relief decoration of its arch spandrels are typical decorative elements of the Mamluk period. This Samaritan niche resembles a classic Mamluk mihrab (prayer niche in a mosque), the model for all domestic niches in the city's houses.

FACING PAGE:

Damascus, Syria, 16th century
Islamic Period
Digital reproduction, I.583

Museum für Islamische Kunst
Photo: Christian Krug

THIS PAGE:

Damascus, Syria, 16th century
Islamic Period
Stone, carved and painted

Vorderasiatisches Museum, VA 3371

Robe

Mesopotamia, or *Bilad al-Rafidayn* (the land between the two rivers Tigris and Euphrates), has always been a rich source of artistic creation. The influence of ancient Assyrian culture can still be seen today in the archaic motifs and patterns in traditional crafts. Women along the Euphrates weave rugs and textiles, using bright colours that contrast with the flat, monochrome terrain of the riverside. Their decoration consists of geometric patterns as well as floral and figurative motifs, including animal and human figures. Many of the patterns contain symbolic meanings: a palm tree symbolizes longevity, a cypress resurrection and three flowers are the symbols of the unity of family.

Long-skirted robes woven out of silk and metal-thread brocades from northeast Syria were primarily used by Iraqi Kurds who live in the mountainous region that borders Syria, Turkey, and Iraq. This robe shows the ancient eye motifs, transformed into a different medium for its apotropaic function. Its role is to provide protection against evil exactly the way its ancient predecessor, the Eye Idol from Tell Brak also on show in this exhibition, did.

Syria, 18th–19th centuries
Wool, metal-thread; Brocade fabric

Marshall and Marilyn R. Wolf Collection, Toronto

Backgammon or Chess Box

Perhaps the most popular board game in Syria, backgammon occupies a special place in the social life of Syrians. Men and women play it at home, in cafés, and in *Sayrans* (nature outings). Boards are usually made of wood and their pieces traditionally of bone but, more recently, of plastic. Historically, Syrian artisans excelled in making luxury backgammon boards of inlaid wood in various materials and diverse geometric shapes.

This specimen, inlaid with colored wood, bone, and mother-of-pearl, is a particularly elegant polyvalent box from the 19th century. Combining boards for various games—backgammon, chess, and checkers—the intricately ornamented box with various polygonal shapes and colors has drawers for the dice and pieces along its borders. Its assembly shows modern influences in the ingenious combination of boards and storage but its layout and the geometric patterns of its polychromous decorative panels, frames, and board outlines represent the peak of a design tradition that evolved across the Islamic world from at least the 15th century onward.

Syria, 19th century
Wood, wood veneers, bone, and mother-of-pearl; inlaid

On loan from the Royal Ontario Museum, 978.273

The Last Supper

Fateh al-Moudarres (Aleppo 1922–1999), was one of the pioneers of modern art in Syria. He studied in Rome, then in Paris, before returning home in the early 1960's to establish his career as a professional artist and art teacher. Inspired by Surrealism, he nonetheless developed his own idiosyncratic approach which, though minimalist and pushing toward abstraction, never relinquished figuration. Personal tragedies that started with the loss of his father before he was even born and culminated in the death of two of his children, as well as an intellectual and political commitment to the great ill-fated causes of his age—nationalism, Palestine, social justice—shaped the subjects of his images and colored their pictorial mood. It is thus no surprise that Jesus Christ and his Passion became a recurrent theme in his art through which he revealed his melancholy, frustrations, and hopes.

Al-Moudarres's Christ emerges as a man of the region, with black hair and dark skin, and the iconic events of his life, like this Last Supper, painted in 1964, are usually set in the vast vistas of the Middle East, with their tonal opacity achieved through thick and layered pigment. They present altered narratives that are reduced to a few signs of the classical canonical scenes: a table and some food items, in this instance. Jesus and his three (female?) companions are minimally represented in a loose geometric fashion, still managing to convey a strong and dynamic humanity. This became al-Moudarres's signature technique, applied to all sorts of historic, mythical, and quotidian scenes, where the composition, colors, and textures conveyed profound emotions and insights that could not be expressed in words.

Fateh al-Moudarres, 1964
Oil on canvas

The Atassi Foundation

Untitled

Aktham Abdul Hamid is one of Syria's leading sculptors. He works in stone and wood as primary materials. His style is contemporary.

According to the artist, the wood sculpture "Untitled" is a Syrian woman dreaming of a better future. The sculpture is characterized by its simplicity of composition. Abdul Hamid makes only limited use of the human body, though his sculptures employ human features and symbols, drawn from the legacy of Syrian sculptural memory.

Aktham Abdul Hamid, 2006
Syrian Walnut

The Atassi Foundation

PARTNER INSTITUTIONS AND OBJECT LIST

LOUVRE MUSEUM, PARIS

Vase
Historic Syria, 3rd millennium BCE
Alabaster gypsum, carved
Department of Near Eastern Antiquities, AO 29723

Seal of Yakhdun-Lim
Mari, Syria, ca. 1800 BCE
Terracotta, engraved
Department of Near Eastern Antiquities, AO 18236

Statuette of a Warrior God
Latakia, northern Syria, 13th century BCE
Bronze
Department of Near Eastern Antiquities, AO 11187

Stele of Teshub
Tell Ahmar, northern Syria, 9th century BCE
Basalt, carved
Department of Near Eastern Antiquities, AO 13091

Vase
Homs, Syria, late 6th century
Silver, hammered, chased and engraved
Department of Greek, Etruscan, and Roman Antiquities, Bj 1895

Fragment of a Floor Mosaic
Daphne (near Antioch), Historic Syria, late 5th–early 6th centuries
Stone and cement
Department of Greek, Etruscan, and Roman Antiquities, Ma 3459

Vase
Made for sultan al-Malik al-Nasir Salah al-Din Yusuf (r. 1236–1260)
Aleppo or Damascus, Syria, 1236–1260
Copper alloy, hammered, repoussé, chased and inlaid with silver and black paste
Department of Islamic Art, OA 4090

THE METROPOLITAN MUSEUM OF ART, NEW YORK

Bowl
Probably Homs, Syria, 25 BCE–25 CE
Glass, mosaic
Rogers Fund, 1912 (12.212.1)

Censer from the Attarouthi Treasure
Attarouthi, Syria, 500–600
Silver, silver-gilt
Purchase, Rogers Fund and Henry J. and Drue E. Heinz
Foundation, Norbert Schimmel, and Lila Acheson Wallace Gifts,
1986 (1986.3.13)

Chalice from the Attarouthi Treasure
Attarouthi, Syria, 500–600
Silver, silver-gilt
Purchase, Rogers Fund and Henry J. and Drue E. Heinz
Foundation, Norbert Schimmel, and Lila Acheson Wallace Gifts,
1986 (1986.3.9)

Chalice from the Attarouthi Treasure
Attarouthi, Syria, 500–600
Silver, silver-gilt
Purchase, Rogers Fund and Henry J. and Drue E. Heinz
Foundation, Norbert Schimmel, and Lila Acheson Wallace Gifts,
1986 (1986.3.10)

Plaque with Saint Paul
Historic Syria, 550–600
Silver, repoussé, chased and gilded
Fletcher Fund, 1950 (50.5.1)

Ewer
Syria, 8th–early 9th centuries
Bronze, cast and pierced
Samuel D. Lee Fund, 1941 (41.65)

Ewer
Raqqa, Syria, late 12th–first half of 13th centuries
Fritware, underglazed and lustre-painted
Henry G. Leberthon Collection, Gift of Mr. and Mrs. A. Wallace
Chauncey, 1957 (57.61.1)

ROYAL ONTARIO MUSEUM, TORONTO

Eye Idol
Tell Brak, Syria, ca. 3200 BCE
Gypsum, carved
Royal Ontario Museum, 959.91.50

Figurine of Seated Male
Ugarit, Syria, 14th–13th centuries BCE
Bronze, cast and gilded
Gift of Hyam M. Smith, 950.83

Lion's Head
Historic Syria, 9th–8th centuries BCE
Ivory, carved
Anonymous Gift; Certified by the Canadian Cultural Property
Export Review Board, 996.86.1

Panel
Nimrud, Historic Syria, 8th century BCE
Ivory, carved
Royal Ontario Museum, 959.91.6

Panel
Historic Syria, 8th–7th centuries BCE
Ivory, carved and inlaid with ceramic
961.13.5

Panel
Historic Syria, 7th century BCE
Ivory, carved
959.91.3

Panel
Nimrud, Historic Syria, 7th century BCE
Ivory, ceramic; carved and inlaid
959.91.5

Tomb Relief
Palmyra, Syria, 100–200
Limestone, carved
953X94.4

Tomb Relief
Palmyra, Syria, 123
Limestone, carved
953X94.1

Flask
Historic Syria, 7th–8th centuries
Glass, free blown and applied
Gift of Miss Helen Norton, 950.157.78

Bowl
Western Syria, late 11th century
Fritware, lustre-painted
960.219.1

Bowl
Western Syria, late 11th century
Fritware, lustre-painted
960.219.3

Bowl
Syria, 13th century
Glass, blown and enamelled
909.31.5

Tile Panel
Damascus, Syria, 16th century
Fritware, underglaze-painted
924.16.127.A-D

Backgammon or Chess Box
Syria, 19th century
Wood, wood veneers, bone, and mother-of-pearl; inlaid
Gift Mr. Denis Slattery, 978.273

STAATLICHE MUSEEN ZU BERLIN, MUSEUM FÜR ISLAMISCHE KUNST, BERLIN

Candlestick
Syria, late 13th century
Copper alloy, cast, chased and inlaid with silver
I. B. 111

Incense burner
Syria, 13th century
Copper alloy, silver and gold, pierced, engraved and inlaid
MIK I. 2774

Niche From a Samaritan House
Damascus, Syria, 16th century
I.583
Photo: Christian Krug

Aleppo Room 17th century (animation)
Aleppo, Styria, dated 1600–01, 1603
Painting on wood
I.2862
Photo: Johannes Kramer

STAATLICHE MUSEEN ZU BERLIN, VORDERASIATISCHES MUSEUM, BERLIN

Relief
Tell Halaf, Syria, 10th–9th centuries BCE
Basalt, carved
Max Freiherr von Oppenheim-Stiftung, Köln, TH B 1497

Relief
Tell Halaf, Syria, 10th–9th centuries BCE
Basalt, carved
Max Freiherr von Oppenheim-Stiftung, Köln, TH B 1490

Stele with Depiction of a Prayer
Tell Halaf, Syria, 10th–9th centuries BCE
Basalt, carved
Max Freiherr von Oppenheim-Stiftung, Köln, TH B 4871

Inscription Panel
Damascus, Syria, 16th century
Stone, carved and painted
VA 3371

THE ATASSI FOUNDATION

Madonna and Child
Probably Homs, Syria, 19th century
Oil on wood

The Last Supper
Fateh Moudarres, 1964
Oil on canvas

Bism Allah al-Rahman al-Rahim
Mahmoud Hammad, 1982
Oil on Canvas

Untitled
Lotfi Al Romhein, 2006
Wood

Untitled
Aktham Abdul Hamid, 2006
Syrian walnut wood

Deluge: The Gods Abandon Palmyra
Elias Zayat, 2011–2012
Acrylic on Canvas

Storeys Series
Tammam Azzam, 2015
Acrylic on Canvas

MARSHALL AND MARILYN R. WOLF COLLECTION, TORONTO

Robe
Syria, 18th–19th centuries
Wool, cotton, silk, metal-thread; woven
Marshall and Marilyn R. Wolf Collection, Toronto

Robe
Syria, 18th–19th centuries
Wool, metal-thread; Brocade fabric
Marshall and Marilyn R. Wolf Collection, Toronto

AGA KHAN MUSEUM, TORONTO

Panel
Damascus, Syria, 17th–18th centuries
Fritware, underglaze-painted
AKM585

Bowl
Made for an officer of Sultan al-Malik al-Nasir Muhammad
b. Qalawun (r. 1293–1341)
Egypt or Syria, first half of 14th century
Brass, inlaid with silver
AKM610

Qur'an Section
Q17: 1-2
Syria or Egypt, mid-14th century
Ink, opaque watercolour, and gold on paper
AKM279

Albarello
Syria, 15th century
Fritware, underglaze-painted
AKM569

CONTRIBUTORS

FILIZ ÇAKIR PHILLIP

Co-Curator, *Syria: A Living History* and Curator, Aga Khan Museum

Filiz Çakır Phillip is Curator at the Aga Khan Museum in Toronto. She studied Art History and Classical Archaeology, Turcology and Museums Management and was awarded a Doctor's degree in Islamic Art History at Freie Universität Berlin. She worked as curator at Museum of Islamic Art, Berlin and has been Senior Fellow at Excellence Cluster TOPOI and Research Fellow at Kunsthistorisches Institut in Florenz—Max-Planck-Society and the Metropolitan Museum of Art, New York. Filiz Çakır Phillip has i.a. published on Islamic archaeology in Ottoman lands, Islamic arms and armour, Islamic book bindings and drawings, including "Enchanted Lines: Drawings from the Aga Khan Museum Collection", a book showcasing the drawings in their historical and artistic context. Her latest book on Iranian arms and armour goes into depth on so far unpublished objects from the two major Islamic arms and armour collections of Berlin, the Museum of Islamic Art and the German Historical Museum.

NASSER RABBAT

Co-Curator, *Syria: A Living History*

Nasser Rabbat is the Aga Khan Professor and the Director of the Aga Khan Program for Islamic Architecture at MIT. An architect and a historian, his scholarly interests include the history and historiography of Islamic architecture, art, and cultures, urban history, modern Arab history, contemporary Arab art, and post-colonial criticism. He has published six books and more than 100 scholarly articles, including *al-Mudun al-Mayyita* *(The Dead Cities)* (2010), a book on this region in Northern Syria that still has the most complete collection of Antique rural architecture in the world. He is currently working on an intellectual biography of the 15th century historian al-Maqrizi. Professor Rabbat regularly contributes to a number of Arabic newspapers on current political and cultural issues and consults with international design firms on urban projects in the Islamic World.

ROSS BURNS

Consultant, *Syria: A Living History*

Ross Burns is the author of three books on the archaeology and history of Syria with a fourth in press. After graduating from Sydney University, he spent almost forty years in the Australian Foreign Service, with assignments in several Middle Eastern countries, including as Ambassador to Syria in the mid-1980s. Since retiring from diplomatic life in 2003, he furthered his education by preparing a doctorate at Macquarie University in Sydney on the archaeology of Roman cities of the Eastern Empire.

The Great Hall Krak de Chevalier
Crusader period
Image courtesy of Ross Burns

First published in Canada in 2016 by
The Aga Khan Museum
77 Wynford Drive
Toronto, Ontario
M3C 1K1
www.agakhanmuseum.org

Publications: Ruba Kana'an, Head of Education and Scholarly Programs, Aga Khan Museum

Editor: Diane Watson
Cover and Interior Design: Martin Gould / martingould.com

ISBN 978 1 926473 07 9

Library and Archives Canada Cataloguing in Publication

Syria : a living history.

Catalogue of an exhibition held at the Aga Khan Museum
    from October 15, 2016 to February 26, 2017.
ISBN 978-1-926473-07-9 (paperback)

    1. Art, Syrian--Exhibitions. 2. Syria--History--Exhibitions.
3. Syria--Civilization--Exhibitions. I. Rabbat, Nasser. Syria.
II. Aga Khan Museum (Toronto, Ont.), issuing body, host institution

DS95.S97 2016   956.91   C2016-906312-7

Photograph Credits

Copyright © Aga Khan Museum, Canada, 2016: page 30.
Copyright © Image courtesy of the Atassi Foundation, UAE, 2016: pages 38, 40.
Copyright © The Musée du Louvre, Dist. RMN-Grand Palais/Paul Veysseyre/Art Resource, NY : pages 24, 26.
Copyright © The Musée du Louvre, Dist. RMN-Drand Palais/Hervé Lewandowski/Art Resource, NY : page 26
Copyright © The Metropolitan Museum of Art, USA, Image source: Art Resource, NY. 2016: page 20.
Copyright © With the Permission of the Royal Ontario Museum, Canada, 2016: pages 13, 14, 18, 22, 36.
Copyright © Staatliche Museen zu Berlin, Museum für Islamische Kunst, Germany, 2016: page 28.
Copyright © Staatliche Museen zu Berlin, Vorderasiatisches Museum, Germany, photo Olaf M. Teßmer, 2016: pages 16, 33.
Copyright © Staatliche Museen zu Berlin, Museum für Islamische Kunst, Germany, photo Christian Krug, 2016: page 28, 32.
Images courtesy of Ross Burns 2016: pages 2, 4, 7, 8, 46 and inner cover.

Care has been taken to trace the ownership of any copyright material used in this book. The publisher welcomes any information enabling it to rectify any references or credits in subsequent editions.

Printed by Andora Graphics Inc. in Canada

INSIDE FRONT AND BACK COVERS:

Interior of the muqarnas Dome
Nuriyya Madrasa
Damascus, 12th century